Science in a flash

States of Matter

Georgia
Amson-Bradshaw

W

Franklin Watts
Published in Great Britain in paperback in 2018 by The Watts Publishing Group

Produced for Franklin Watts by
White-Thomson Publishing Ltd
www.wtpub.co.uk

Credits
Series Editor: Georgia Amson-Bradshaw
Series Designer: Rocket Design (East Anglia) Ltd

The publisher would like to thank the following for permission to reproduce their pictures:
Images from shutterstock: karpenko_ilia 4tr, 4t, Elvetica 6, MO_SES Premium 8b, ImagePixel 8r, Nenov Brothers
Images 9t, hans.slegers 9b, egg design 10t, TFoxFoto 11tr, Photo Melon 12t, Zilu8 13t, GraphicsRF 14, Javier
Brosch 14br, Lorelyn Medina 15, Vladimir Sazonov 16b, Lucie Lang 17bl, Mamuka
Gotsiridze 17br, Artisticco 18, geniuscook_com 20c, Guingm 20bl Creative Nature
Media 22l, Macrovector 23b, GraphicsRF 24b nobeastsofierce 27t
Images from other sources: SecretDisc wiki commons 26b
Illustrations by Steve Evans: 5br, 6r, 7l, 11br, 12b, 14bl, 15c, 17t, 18b, 19b, 23br, 25br, 27br
All design elements from Shutterstock.

Every attempt has been made to clear copyright. Should there be any inadvertent omission
please apply to the publisher for rectification.

PB ISBN 978 1 4451 5273 8

Printed in China

Franklin Watts
An imprint of
Hachette Children's Group
Part of The Watts Publishing Group
Carmelite House
50 Victoria Embankment
London EC4Y 0DZ

An Hachette UK Company
www.hachette.co.uk

www.franklinwatts.co.uk

In this book you'll
see some words
shown in **bold**.
These are described
on the glossary
page at the back of
the book .

Adult supervision is
required when carrying
out the experiments in
this book.

Contents

MATERIALS AND MATTER

Everything in the world is made from matter.

Matter is what we call all stuff. If you can feel it, smell it or taste it, it is matter. Even things you can't see, such as air and other **gases**, are made of matter.

What's the matter?

Everything! It's all matter...

BUILDING BLOCKS

All matter is made up of **atoms**, which are the tiny building blocks of all stuff. If you kept dividing a gold coin into smaller and smaller bits, eventually you would end up with one atom of gold: the smallest bit of gold possible.

MOLECULES

Sometimes atoms join together into groups called **molecules**. Joining atoms into molecules often forms the smallest building block of a new **material**. For example, the smallest building block of water is a single water molecule.

GOLD!

GOLD   GOLD ATOM   WATER   WATER MOLECULE

ZOOM   ZOOM

MATERIAL WORLD

Material is the word for a particular type of matter. Water is a material, and so are rubber, plastic, wood and steel. Materials can be described by their **properties**, such as hardness, softness or transparency.

WATER

WOOD

HOUSE

DESIRABLE PROPERTIES

The properties of different materials make them useful for different things. For example, buildings are often made of hard, strong materials to stop them from falling down.

Riddle me this!

Buildings are normally made from strong, hard materials. But why might buildings in earthquake-prone areas often be built with soft, flexible materials, like rubber, in their foundations?

Answer on page 28.

Did you know?

Diamond is the hardest natural material in the world. The only thing that can scratch a diamond is another diamond!

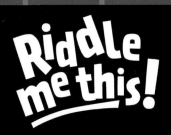

STATES OF MATTER

Matter can be a solid, a liquid or a gas.

Look around you at the different types of matter or materials that you can see and feel. A solid wooden table perhaps? A glass of water? The air blowing in and out of your lungs? All materials can be divided up into three main **states of matter: solid, liquid,** and gas.

Changing states

Some materials can easily change between the three states. For example, water can be a solid (ice), a liquid, or a gas (water vapour). These changes can be reversed by heating or cooling.

gas
(water vapour)

liquid
(water)

solid (ice)

POP QUIZ!

Which of these is an example of a liquid:

a) Salt

b) Jelly

c) Oil

Answer on page 28.

Cooking with chemistry

We often change the states of materials in the kitchen. We put liquid juice in the freezer to make solid ice lollies. We **melt** solid butter into a liquid on the stove to fry things in.

ARGH! Look at the state of your hat!

FACT ATTACK

There is a fourth state of matter called **plasma** but it is very unusual. It is created when the atoms in a gas start to break down. Plasma television screens contain plasma.

Irreversible changes

Not all materials change back and forth between states like water can. Wood or cotton fabrics that are heated don't become liquid – they **burn**. These sorts of changes are not reversible. Learn more about **irreversible** changes on page 24.

7

All about solids

Solids keep their shape.

Solid objects are kind of like the sturdy, sensible ones in the gang: they always keep themselves together, and stay in shape. This is because the particles (the atoms or molecules) that make up a solid are very tightly bonded, and they stick firmly together.

Yeaahh, I like to stay in shape.

Particles in a solid hold firmly together.

Some materials that are solid are very hard, like brick.

Solid materials can be natural or man-made. Wood is a natural material. Plastic is a man-made material.

Some solids, like butter, are soft and can be squashed into a new shape, but they do not flow.

Solids don't change shape if you turn them upside down, or put them into a new container.

Solids have a fixed **volume**. This means they always take up the same amount of space, even if they change shape.

Some solid materials, such as sand, are **powders**. Powders can behave a little differently to other solids. This is because they are made up of lots of tiny pieces of solid material. Each individual piece behaves like a normal solid, but when they are all added together they can flow, like a liquid.

Sponges can seem like they have a smaller volume when they are squashed. But in fact, the solid part of the sponge keeps the same volume. It is air spaces inside the sponge that get pushed out, making it seem smaller.

Did you know?

The lightest solid in the world is a man-made material called aerogel. It contains 99.98 per cent air!

All about liquids

Liquids change shape easily, but always have the same volume.

You could say liquids are a bit more easy-going than solids. The particles that make up a liquid are connected more loosely than in a solid, and in a more random arrangement. This lets the particles jiggle past each other, so a liquid can flow.

I just go with the flow, man...

Fixed volume

Although liquids don't have a fixed shape, they do have a fixed volume. A liquid will take up the same amount of space even if the container is changed.

Particles in a liquid have looser bonds than in a solid.

250 ml

200

150

100

50

75 ml

75 ml

The amount of liquid is the same, but the shape is different.

Liquid properties

Like solids, liquids can have different textures and properties. Some flow more easily than others. Water flows more easily than thick, sticky honey, for example. The word for this is **viscosity**.

That's heavy, dude

Some liquids are more **dense** than others. Denser liquids are heavier, so if you put them in a container they form layers with the heavier, denser liquids at the bottom and the lighter ones on top. You can see this happen when petrol is spilled on wet ground. The petrol floats on top of the water, and light refracts through, creating a rainbow.

Give it a go!

Make a groovy shakeable liquid density column. You'll need a jug, water, vegetable oil, rubbing **alcohol** (70% or 91%), natural sea salt, food colouring (green is good) and a clear plastic bottle or jar with a lid.

First, mix water and salt together in the jug. Keep adding salt and mixing until new salt added won't **dissolve**.

Pour some of this salty water into the clear bottle, until it is one-third full. Next, add oil, until it is two-thirds full. Finally, pour the alcohol into the bottle until it is nearly full.

Add a few drops of food colouring to the bottle, and shake. The three layers should mix together. But what happens when you set the bottle down?

Shake ... and settle

All about gases

Gases have no fixed volume and spread out to fill any space.

Gases are the crazy ones of the bunch. Their particles are not connected, so they whizz about in all directions, full of **energy**. Because of this, a gas will always expand to fill a space.

Feel the flow

Gases can flow very easily. Wind is a flow of gas. Fans and hair-dryers create gas flows to do work like cooling us down or drying things out.

Particles in a gas are very spread out and can move in all directions.

I'm a laughing gas!

Did you know?

Gases are all around us, all the time, but most of them are invisible and have no smell.

No fixed volume

Unlike solids and liquids, gases don't have a fixed volume. A small amount of gas put into a big container will simply spread out to fill the container. Gases can also be **compressed** very easily.

Hot air in the balloon is lighter than the air outside.

How do we come down?

Feel the heat

Heating a material up gives more energy to its particles. So the particles in a hot gas will whizz around with even more speed and energy than when cold. This makes the gas spread out further, or increase in volume. Because the particles are spread out further, a hot gas is also less dense, and less heavy than a cold gas. This is how hot air balloons work: by making the air in the balloon lighter than the air outside.

Give it a go!

See how temperature affects the volume of a gas. You will need a balloon, a sewing tape measure, pen and paper and a freezer.

Blow up the balloon and tie it off. Measure around it at its fattest point.

Record the size of your balloon, then put it in the freezer for two hours.

Now, remove your balloon and immediately measure around it again. What do you notice?

2 HOURS

Melting and Freezing

A solid 'melts' when it warms into a liquid.

A liquid 'freezes' when it cools into a solid.

We know that by heating or cooling many materials it is possible to change their states. A solid that is heated up goes soft and loses its fixed shape. It melts or turns into a liquid. A liquid that is cooled down **freezes** into a solid.

Heat energy from the Sun

It's all about the energy

The reason solids melt is because heating matter gives extra energy to the particles. While the atoms have less energy they stay fairly still, but adding energy makes them jiggle around more and more. Finally the extra energy makes the strong bonds between the particles break down, and the particles can move more freely.

The point at which a solid turns to a liquid is called its **melting point.**

Am I melting, or just sweating?

14

Frozen solid

Freezing is the same process as melting but in reverse. As liquid is cooled, heat energy is taken away, and the particles move around less. Eventually they stay still and form a fixed shape. The temperature at which this happens is called the **freezing point.**

Hot enough to melt?

It seems odd when you first think about it, but most metals are frozen when at room temperature! For example, the metal aluminium melts at 660.3 degrees Celsius, so at room temperature, which is about 20 degrees Celsius, aluminium is in its solid, frozen state. In contrast, sunflower oil has a melting point of -17 degrees Celsius, so is liquid at room temperature.

Riddle me this!

If the freezing point of water is zero degrees Celsius, what is water's melting point?
Answer on page 28.

Evaporating, boiling and condensing

Liquids evaporate or boil to become a gas. Gases condense into a liquid.

Heating and cooling can also change liquids to gases and back again. Just like with melting and freezing, it's all to do with how much energy the atoms have, and how much they whizz around.

Boiling

The most dramatic way a liquid becomes a gas is if it **boils**. This is when a liquid is heated to a high temperature, and the particles absorb so much energy that bubbles form throughout the liquid, as the whole body of the liquid is turning into a gas at once. The temperature that this happens at is called the **boiling point**.

The boiling point of water is 100 degrees Celsius.

POP QUIZ!

Which of these three things would NOT make a puddle of water **evaporate** faster:

a) Sunny weather

b) Windy weather

c) Humid weather

Answer on page 28.

Gasp, now I need to drink some water!

FACT ATTACK

Cool it!

Our bodies use evaporation to cool us down. Heat energy is carried away from our bodies by our sweat changing from a liquid to a gas.

Evaporation

A liquid doesn't have to boil to become a gas. It can evaporate into a gas at cooler temperatures too, but the difference is evaporation only happens at the liquid's surface. Think of the steam rising from a hot cup of tea. At the liquid's surface, the particles are only being held on to the other particles from one side. As a result, it's easier for them to break away and float off as a gas.

Condensation

The opposite of evaporation is **condensation**. This is when particles of a gas lose energy and reform into a liquid. You can see this happen when you breathe onto a cold window or take a cold can out of the fridge. The water vapour in the air is cooled by touching the cold can, and it forms droplets of liquid.

THE WATER CYCLE

Water on Earth is constantly changing from a liquid to a gas and back again.

Water is an unusual material. At the temperatures we normally experience on Earth, most materials are either a solid, liquid, or gas, and generally they stay that way. Water is an exception, in that we regularly find water in all three states: frozen as ice, as a liquid we can drink, or as vapour in the air.

Life giver

The **water cycle** (steps 1–3 in this picture) supports most life on Earth. It provides fresh water, which plants rely on to grow. Plants feed animals (including humans) who also drink the fresh water from the lakes and rivers.

1

Water from oceans and lakes evaporates into the sky, to form clouds of water vapour (a gas).

Did you know?

70 per cent of the Earth's surface is covered with water, but 97 per cent of that is saltwater in the oceans that we cannot drink.

2

Clouds rise into cold air, causing the vapour to condense into liquid rain.

3

Rain falls onto the land, and runs into lakes and the ocean. The cycle begins again.

Give it a go!

Make your own mini model of the water cycle. You'll need a large metal or plastic bowl, cling film, a mug, a long piece of string or large rubber band, a small weight such as a small stone or pencil sharpener, and some water.

Fill the large bowl with water until it is about a quarter full. Place the mug in the centre of the bowl in the water, but make sure the mug is dry on the inside.

Cover the top of the bowl with cling film, and hold it in place with string or the rubber band. Put the small weight directly in the centre of the cling film, so it makes a small dip in the plastic over the mug.

Put the bowl in a sunny spot outside and leave it there for about an hour, then move it carefully into the shade. What do you see? Read about it on page 29.

rubber band   small weight   cling film

water level

19

WHAT is a MIXTURE?

When materials are combined together, they make a mixture.

Mixtures can be solids, liquids, or gases. Most of the objects we find in our day-to-day lives are made up of different materials mixed together.

A mixed picture

Sometimes a mixture is obvious, because the bits of each material are big enough to see. Think of a piece of rocky road – the bits of biscuit, marshmallow and chocolate are all different materials, so the mixture is easily visible.

I have conducted rigorous scientific tests and analysis shows this cake IS a mixture.

Scientific analysis tells me this salty water tastes gross!

Invisible ingredients

It's not always obvious just from looking if something is a mixture. Saltwater, for example, doesn't look like a mixture because you can't see the separate molecules of salt and water.

A mix of mixtures

Mixtures come in two main types, which have the fancy names of a 'heterogeneous mixture' and a 'homogeneous mixture'.

A '**HETEROGENEOUS MIXTURE**' is a mixture like rocky road – the different bits are not evenly spread. Other examples of this type of mixture are noodle soup, salad and chocolate chip cookies.

In a '**HOMOGENEOUS MIXTURE**' like saltwater, the bits are evenly distributed. These sorts of mixtures are also called **solutions**. Examples are vinegar and wine.

Does it dissolve?

You can make a solution by dissolving one material in another, such as sugar in tea. If a material dissolves in liquid to make a solution, we say it is **soluble**. If it doesn't dissolve, like sand in water, we say it is **insoluble**.

I told you before, I don't take sugar in my tea!

POP QUIZ!

Which of these three things is a homogeneous mixture, and which are heterogeneous mixtures:

a) Pizza   b) Sugar syrup   c) Soil

Answer on page 29.

SEPARATING MIXTURES

Mixtures can be separated using filtration or distillation.

Mixtures are often useful or necessary, but sometimes we need to separate the different materials in a mixture. How we do this depends on the type of mixture we want to separate.

Simple filters

Sometimes a mixture is quite easy to separate. Think about when you boil a saucepan of peas in water. When the peas are ready, you pour the mixture of peas and water through a colander or sieve. This is a form of **filtration**. The sieve is a filter – it only lets the water through, and keeps the peas behind.

Filter

Separate solids

Filtration can be used for other mixtures too. A mixture of solids, such as sand and pebbles, can be poured through a sieve so the larger pebbles are held behind. Sometimes it is necessary to use a filter with very small gaps, like a piece of filter paper. Filter paper will let water pass, but can stop tiny solids like grains of sand.

Solution: distillation!

Filtration doesn't work with solutions like sugar water where the molecules are spread throughout the mixture and are too small to be filtered. To separate a solution we use a process called **distillation**. Distillation works by evaporating the water, and leaving the dissolved material (such as sugar) behind.

Riddle me this!

Think about what you know about different liquids' boiling points. Do you think it is possible to separate a mixture of liquids, such as water and alcohol? How could you do it?

Answer on page 29.

2. Only the water evaporates

3. The water cools and condenses again

Mixture

1. The mixture is heated

HA HA, I have the solution!

IRREVERSIBLE CHANGES

Changes in some materials cannot be undone.

Not every material is like water – able to change between the three different states of matter. While some materials can melt and refreeze over and over again, some material changes can only happen once. These are called irreversible changes.

What's cookin'?

Think about frying an egg in a pan: it starts off as a gloopy liquid, then turns into a solid when it is cooked. But cooling it down doesn't turn it back into a raw egg again. This is because heating it has caused chemical changes inside it that cannot be undone.

Feel the burn

Burning is also a type of irreversible change. Heating wood creates smoke and ash, which cannot be changed back into wood.

EYE SPY!

The eggs have cooked and the wood has burned. But can you spot another irreversible change in this picture?

Chemical combinations

Irreversible changes don't just come from heating materials – mixing substances can cause irreversible changes too. For example, mixing bicarbonate of soda with an acid, such as vinegar, releases bubbles of carbon dioxide that cannot be turned back into bicarbonate of soda and vinegar again.

Give it a go!

Be a rocket scientist! You'll need a 500 ml plastic drinks bottle and a cork or rubber stopper that fits it, duct tape, three pencils, white vinegar, a tissue, and some bicarbonate of soda.

Tape the three pencils to the drinks bottle so they create 'legs', with the bottle neck pointing downwards. Then turn the bottle upright, and half fill it with vinegar.

Peel your tissue's layers apart so you are left with a single layer. Spoon a heaped tablespoon of bicarbonate of soda onto it. Gently wrap the tissue up around the powder into a slim package.

GO OUTSIDE! Now put the tissue full of bicarb into the bottle, immediately shove the stopper into the top, give the bottle one hard shake, then stand the rocket upright on the pencil legs. Whoosh!

What change has happened here?
Answer on page 29.

tape

pencil legs

tissue

... 3, 2, 1
BLAST OFF!

stopper

The Future of Materials

Scientists are always developing new types of materials.

Throughout history, from the Stone Age, to the modern era of plastics, humankind's use and understanding of materials has transformed how we live our lives. So what new materials will change our lives next?

Would you wear spider silk pants?

Chemical copy-cats

Nature itself has created some of the most impressive materials on the planet, such as spider silk. A spider's web is stronger than steel at the same thickness, and can stretch up to five times without breaking. Scientists have been working on copying spider silk to make this incredible material synthetically.

Metal foam

We use plastic foam, such as **polystyrene**, for packaging because it is light and absorbs energy. But how about metal foam? This new material is super light, but also super strong. In fact, it behaves a lot like human bone. New bone cells can grow around it, so it can be used as a medical implant within a skeleton.

metal foam

Great graphene

Perhaps the biggest advance in material science since the invention of plastic has been the development of graphene. This amazing material is just one atom thick! It is the strongest, lightest, best electricity-conducting material ever created. A sheet the size of a football pitch would weigh less than a single gram.

Crackless concrete?

Concrete is the world's most widely-used building material. It is cheap, strong, and can be shaped into whatever design you choose. But over time, heat and rainwater cause cracks. Enter self-healing concrete. Designed by Dutch scientists, it contains limestone-producing bacteria that are activated when rainwater seeps into the structure, filling the cracks up again.

Concrete buildings like this temple could fix themselves!

Did you know?

Scientists who investigate the properties of materials are called materials scientists.

And the answer is...

Page 5

Riddle me this: Buildings in earthquake-prone areas will often have flexible materials, such as rubber, in their foundations. These squashy materials can absorb the forces from the earthquake, rather than transferring them to the building which might then crack and fall.

Page 6

Pop quiz: The answer is c), oil is a liquid.

Page 15

Riddle me this: If the freezing point of water is zero degrees Celsius then the melting point is ... also zero degrees! It's simply that freezing happens when a material is cooling down, and melting happens when a material is warming up.

Page 16

Pop quiz: The answer is c), humid weather would NOT make a puddle evaporate faster. Wind evaporates puddles by carrying away air that has become full of water vapour, replacing it with dry air that can hold more water molecules.

Page 19

Give it a go: You should see drops of water condensing on the cling film. These then drop as 'rain' into the mug.

Page 21

Pop quiz: a) pizza and c) soil are heterogeneous mixtures. b) sugar syrup is a homogeneous mixture.

Page 23

Riddle me this: One way to separate liquids is by making use of their different boiling points. Alcohol has a lower boiling point than water, so if the two are mixed together you can heat the mixture and the alcohol will evaporate first. The alcohol vapour can then be collected, cooled and condensed back into a liquid. Ta da! You have separated the water and the alcohol.

Page 24

Eye spy!: The other object that has undergone an irreversible change is the rusty can. Rusting is another type of irreversible chemical change. Certain metals will rust when they come into contact with water and oxygen.

Page 25

Give it a go: By mixing the vinegar and bicarbonate of soda, a chemical reaction has taken place and a new material, carbon dioxide gas, has been created.

Glossary

Alcohol A colourless flammable liquid

Atom A tiny building block that everything in the universe is made of

Boil When a liquid gets so hot it turns into a gas, with bubbles forming throughout

Boiling point The temperature at which a particular liquid starts to boil

Burn A chemical change where a material breaks down because of heat

Compress When something is squashed together making it smaller

Condensation The process where a gas cools and becomes a liquid

Dense When the particles of a material are closely packed together

Dissolve When a solid mixes with a liquid completely so it becomes part of the liquid

Distillation A process for separating out mixtures by evaporating liquid

Energy The ability or power to do work

Evaporate Changing from a liquid to a gas at a lower temperature than the boiling point

Filtration Separating mixtures by passing them through a filter ,which keeps one or more parts of the mixture behind

Freeze When a liquid turns into a solid

Freezing point The temperature at which a particular liquid turns into a solid

Gas A material that has no fixed volume or shape, such as air. One of the three main states of matter

Insoluble Will not dissolve when put into a liquid

Irreversible Cannot be undone

Liquid A material that has a fixed volume and can flow, such as water. One of the three main states of matter

Material A particular type of matter, or stuff

Matter The word for all physical 'stuff' in the universe

Melt When a solid turns into a liquid

Melting point The temperature at which a particular solid turns into a liquid

Mixture When materials are combined together

Molecule A group of atoms that have joined up

Plasma The fourth, very rare, state of matter

Powder A material made of lots of tiny little bits of a solid

Polystyrene A type of plastic used to make foam packaging

Property A characteristic of a material, such as being hard or soft, or being able to conduct electricity

Solid A material with a fixed shape, such as ice. One of the three main states of matter

Soluble Will dissolve if put into a liquid such as water

Solution A mixture where one of the substances dissolves in the other

State (of matter) One of the forms that matter can exist in: solid, liquid, gas and occasionally plasma

Viscosity How runny a liquid is

Volume How much space a material fills up

Water cycle The movement of water on Earth between the air, the land, and the ocean

Further reading

Matter: Moving Up With Science
Peter Riley (Franklin Watts)

Materials: Project Science
Sally Hewitt (Franklin Watts)

Materials and Properties: Straight Forward with Science
Peter Riley (Franklin Watts)

Websites

www.bbc.co.uk/education/topics/zryycdm
Video clips all about materials

www.exploratorium.edu/snacks/subject/materials-matter
Fun experiments to do at home

www.explainthatstuff.com/states-of-matter.html
Detailed information about states of matter

Index